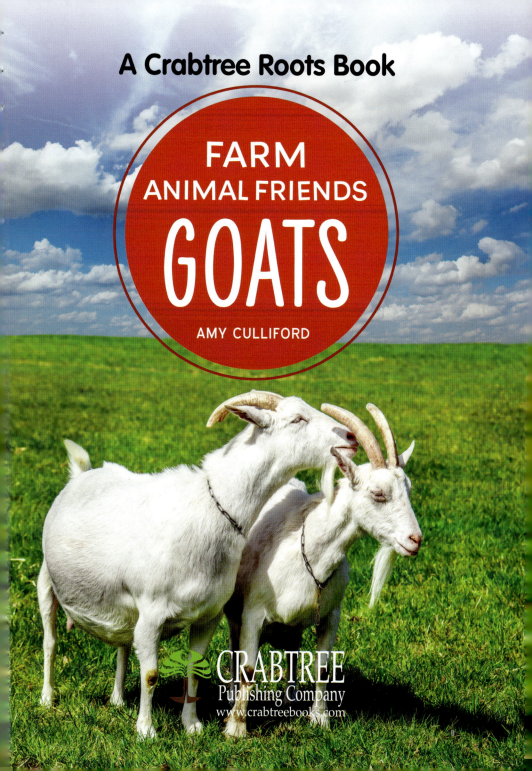

A Crabtree Roots Book

FARM ANIMAL FRIENDS
GOATS

AMY CULLIFORD

CRABTREE
Publishing Company
www.crabtreebooks.com

School-to-Home Support for Caregivers and Teachers

This book helps children grow by letting them practice reading. Here are a few guiding questions to help the reader with building his or her comprehension skills. Possible answers appear here in red.

Before Reading:
- What do I think this book is about?
    - *This book is about goats.*
    - *This book is about goats on farms.*

- What do I want to learn about this topic?
    - *I want to learn what goats eat.*
    - *I want to learn what colors a goat can be.*

During Reading:
- I wonder why…
    - *I wonder why goats like to eat hay.*
    - *I wonder why goats like to jump.*

- What have I learned so far?
    - *I have learned that goats can be different colors.*
    - *I have learned that some goats make milk.*

After Reading:
- What details did I learn about this topic?
    - *I have learned that goats can be white or brown.*
    - *I have learned that goats like to eat hay.*

- Read the book again and look for the vocabulary words.
    - *I see the word **hay** on page 8 and the word **milk** on page 10. The other vocabulary words are found on page 14.*

This is a **goat**.

Some goats are white.

Some goats are brown.

Goats like to eat **hay**.

Some goats make **milk**.

All goats like to jump!

Word List

Sight Words

a	like	this
all	make	to
are	jump	white
brown	is	
eat	some	

Words to Know

goat

hay

milk

26 Words

This is a **goat**.

Some goats are white.

Some goats are brown.

Goats like to eat **hay**.

Some goats make **milk**.

All goats like to jump!

Written by: Amy Culliford
Designed by: Rhea Wallace
Series Development: James Earley
Proofreader: Kathy Middleton
Educational Consultant: Christina Lemke M.Ed.

Photographs:
Shutterstock: fs24: cover (tl); Nataliia Melnychuk: cover (tr); oorka: cover (b); 2xSamara.com: p. 1; Khort Esther Tatiana: p. 3, 14; Anton Havelaar: p. 4; Gelphi: p. 7; Janis Petranis: p. 9, 14; DenysR: p. 10-11, 14; Grigorita Ko: p.13

Library and Archives Canada Cataloguing in Publication
Title: Goats / Amy Culliford.
Names: Culliford, Amy, 1992- author.
Description: Series statement: Farm animal friends | "A Crabtree roots book".
Identifiers: Canadiana (print) 20200382608 | Canadiana (ebook) 20200382616 | ISBN 9781427134523 (hardcover) | ISBN 9781427132475 (softcover) | ISBN 9781427132536 (HTML)
Subjects: LCSH: Goats—Juvenile literature.
Classification: LCC SF383.35 .C85 2021 | DDC j636.3/9—dc23

Library of Congress Cataloging-in-Publication Data
Names: Culliford, Amy, 1992- author.
Title: Goats / Amy Culliford.
Description: New York : Crabtree Publishing Company, 2021. | Series: Farm animal friends : a Crabtree roots book | Includes index. | Audience: Ages 4-6 | Audience: Grades K-1 | Summary: "Early readers are introduced to goats and life on a farm. Simple sentences accompany engaging pictures"-- Provided by publisher.
Identifiers: LCCN 2020049876 (print) | LCCN 2020049877 (ebook) | ISBN 9781427134523 (hardcover) | ISBN 9781427132475 (paperback) | ISBN 9781427132536 (ebook)
Subjects: LCSH: Goats--Juvenile literature. | Livestock--Juvenile literature.
Classification: LCC SF383.35 .C85 2021 (print) | LCC SF383.35 (ebook) | DDC 636.3/9--dc23
LC record available at https://lccn.loc.gov/2020049876
LC ebook record available at https://lccn.loc.gov/2020049877

Crabtree Publishing Company
www.crabtreebooks.com   1-800-387-7650

Printed in the U.S.A./022021/CG20201130

Copyright © 2021 **CRABTREE PUBLISHING COMPANY**

All rights reserved. No part of this publication may be reproduced, stored in a retrieval system or be transmitted in any form or by any means, electronic, mechanical, photocopying, recording, or otherwise, without the prior written permission of Crabtree Publishing Company. In Canada: We acknowledge the financial support of the Government of Canada through the Canada Book Fund for our publishing activities.

Published in the United States
Crabtree Publishing
347 Fifth Avenue, Suite 1402-145
New York, NY, 10016

Published in Canada
Crabtree Publishing
616 Welland Ave.
St. Catharines, Ontario L2M 5V6